JOHN PAUL
THE GREAT

BONECHI

Editorial project: Casa Editrice Bonechi
Editorial management: Alberto Andreini, Monica Bonechi, Serena de Leonardis.
Graphic design and layout by: Manuela Ranfagni
Texts: Comunità di San Leolino, Patrizia Fabbri
Editors: Anna Baldini, Rita Bianucci, Patrizia Fabbri
Technical consultant: Vittorio Benvenuti
Translation by Eve Leckey
The English Bible texts are taken from The New American Bible, USCCB.
Pp. 22, 53, The Poetry of John Paul II, Roman Triptych, USCCB.
The translations of the encyclicals, speeches etc. of the Pope were taken from the official
Vatican website, except for those on pp. 25, 46 translated by Eve Leckey.

Photo credits
The photographs are taken from the archive of Casa Editrice Bonechi.
Most of these were provided by Arturo Mari, Osservatore Romano.
The photographs on the pages indicated below belong to the following agencies:
Adnkronos: pp. 86, 87 below, 90, 92, 93, 94, 95 above
Associated Press: pp. 12-13, 24 below, 25, 28 (Arturo Mari),
30-31, 38 (Victor Ruiz Caballero), 39 above (Arturo Mari), below (Jerome Delay)
40 above left (Arturo Mari), below (Massimo Sambucetti),
41 (Daniel Hulshizer), 55 and 56 (Plinio Lepri), 57 above
(Victor Ruiz Caballero), 57 below (Broglio), 59 (Ron Frehm),
60 (Efrem Lukatsky), 61 (Bruno Mari), 68 above right
(Paulo Duarte), 69, 74 (Andrew Medichini), 75 (Arturo Mari),
78 (Broglio), 79 (Massimo Sambucetti), 80-81
(Marty Lederhandler), 82 (Paolo Cocco), 83 (Gregory Bull),
84 (Eric Draper), 85 (Gregory Bull), 87 above (Luca Bruno),
88-89 (Alessandra Tarantino), 91, 95 below (AP/Osservatore Romano)
Press Photo: pp. 3, 4 below, 5, 6, 7 above, 17, 18, 19, 24 above, 43, 52
Maria Novella Batini: p. 76 below left

Casa Editrice Bonechi
Via dei Cairoli 18/b
50131 Firenze - Italy
tel. 055-576841   fax. 055-5000766
e-mail: bonechi@bonechi.it

Printed in Italy by Centro Stampa Editoriale Bonechi,
Sesto Fiorentino (Firenze)

Website: www.bonechi.com

John Paul II
A pope for two millennia

"The duty of the new Pope will be to introduce the Church into the Third Millennium." These were the words that the then primate of Poland, Cardinal Stefan Wyszynski, archbishop of Warsaw, addressed to Pope John Paul II just a few minutes after his election on 16 October 1978. Words that the Pope himself remembered in his testament thus revealing he had accepted them as an indication that prepared him for the task that lay ahead. And the chronological facts confirmed the statement without a shadow of doubt: as he opened the Holy Door of St Peter's Basilica on Christmas night 1999, John Paul II did indeed introduce the Church into the new millennium. Cardinal Wyszynski's prophecy did not, however, refer simply to an event marked up on the calendar. More than anything, it referred to the spiritual challenge that the Church would have to face over the years to come. For while it was easy to imagine that given its strength and internal order the institution of the Church of Rome would be able to survive for much longer, it was less obvious that it would be able to confront the new millennium without losing its credibility and pertinence to history and within the world, even its vital role and faith in itself. Its position and authority could not at all be taken for granted if we remember the situation as it was in the late 1970s.

When John Paul II acceded to the papal throne,

the Church was in a dramatic state to say the least. Just a year earlier one of the most important scholars of religious affairs, the French writer Jean Delumeau, had published a book with the significant title, *Le christianisme va-t-il mourir?* (Is Christianity dying?). The anthropological revolution that had emerged in 1968 seemed to have shaken to its roots the existence and identity of the Christian faith, especially in the western world: protest hit the Church hard and sociologists could do no more than register the amazing extent of the process of secularization that caused a drastic reduction in the number of the faithful. The crisis in the priesthood seemed, moreover, to indicate the beginning of the end for the traditional model of the Catholic Church, to such an extent that a crisis in the body itself was openly discussed. Only ten years from its conclusion, the conflict between reformers and conservatives began to threaten the Second Vatican Council: some accused the Council of having provoked the current crisis, while others felt it was already out of date and obsolete. Moreover, the papacy of Paul VI that had providentially completed a great process of renewal within the Church, closed dramatically at precisely the same moment as the kidnap and murder of Aldo Moro, a respected Italian politician.

The outlook was no less troubled on the social and politcal levels. The contrasts between the two power blocks that divided the world at the time reached moments of high drama, the most striking of which was the attempted assassination of John Paul II in the square of St Peter's on 13 May 1981, not very long after the start of his pontificate. There was still a strong and genuine risk of nuclear war, while at the same time the threat of global pollution, frequently referred to by the Pope, was increasing and disturbing the conscience of the most perceptive. Other pressing issues were the problems of those countries which had recently emerged from colonial rule, the deepening disparity between north and south and the emergence of the first oil crisis: these were all challenges that demanded of the Church a renewed commitment and perhaps also a new way of approaching and dealing with them. Indeed, following Paul VI and after the brief period of the papacy of Albino Luciani, the Church inherited a far from easy situation. Throughout western society in those years all sectors experienced a negative reflex movement following the sharp forward thrust of the economic boom.

It was in this situation that the Cardinal of Krakow at the age of just 58, rose to the papacy. And he brought to it all that he had, just like the apostle Peter when, as he entered the temple to pray after the resurrection of Christ, he heard the voice of a man crippled from birth asking for charity. "And Peter, fastening his eyes upon him with John, said, Look on us. And he gave heed unto them, expecting to receive something of them. Then Peter said, Silver and gold have I none; but such as I have give I thee: In the name of Jesus Christ of Nazareth rise up and walk. And he took him by the right hand, and lifted him up: and immediately his feet and ankle bones received strength. And he leaping up stood, and walked, and entered with them into the temple, walking, and leaping, and praising God." (Acts 3, 4-8). And it was the name of Jesus Christ that John Paul II announced, almost shouting it, in that memorable first homily of 22 October 1978, "Brothers and sisters, do not be afraid to welcome Christ and accept his power. Help the Pope and all those who wish to serve Christ and with Christ's power to serve the human person and the whole of mankind. Do not be afraid. Open wide the doors for Christ. To his saving power open the boundaries of States, economic and political systems, the vast fields of culture, civilization and development. Do not be afraid. Christ knows "what is in man". He alone knows it. So often today man does not know what is within him, in the depths of his mind and heart. So often he is uncertain about the meaning of his life on this earth. He is assailed by doubt, a doubt which turns into despair. We ask you therefore, we beg you with humility and trust, let Christ speak to man. He alone has words of life, yes, of eternal life."

It is a cry, a plea that continued and was repeated right until the end, throughout his entire pontificate, like a guiding light in this ministry of evangelization, witness and renewal that John Paul carried throughout the world never sparing either thought or care for himself. It is a cry that still resounds undiminished in the last great programme document officially published at the end of the great Jubilee year, 2000, the Apostolic Letter *Novo Millennio Ineunte*. Here, once again John Paul invited the Church to open its heart and go forward, entering the third millennium with hope, "*Duc in altum!* Let us go forward in hope! A new millennium is opening before the Church like a vast ocean upon which we shall venture, relying on the help of Christ." (58) And he added, confirming the call to its mission and almost exhorting the church to rediscover its own youthfulness, still fresh after two thousand years of history, "At the beginning of this new century, our steps must quicken as we travel the highways of the world" because, "it is not to a dull everyday routine that we return. On the contrary, if ours has been a genuine pilgrimage, it will have as it were stretched our legs for the journey still ahead. (59)

Continually recalling the Church to this voyage, John Paul II was himself its able helmsman. He went forward with his sights always firmly fixed on the compass that he had chosen "to direct us on the journey of the century that is opening", in other words the second Vatican Council which the Pope defined as "the great gift that has benefited the Church in the 20th century". The future of the Church lay within the Council: this is, in fact, the most profound spiritual heritage of his papacy, strongly asserted in one of the key passages of his Testament, "I am convinced that for a long time to come the new generations will draw upon the riches that this Council of the 20th century gave us. As a bishop who participated in this conciliar event from the first to the last day, I wish to entrust this great patrimony to all those who are and who will be called in the future to realize it. For my part I thank the eternal Pastor Who allowed me to serve this very great cause during the course of all the years of my pontificate." Indeed, it is possible to understand and interpret the wide horizons of John Paul's pontificate as the result of his generous and tireless service to the council's programme. It is precisely that one hundred per cent dedication that has lead many to take up the title that history has attributed to very few popes: John Paul the Great.

The Council is a three-dimensional image of the Church, a comprehensive way of working, an effort to synthesize the sacrosant aspects of Christian life, as described in the four great constitutions of the Council: liturgy, the word of God, the identity of the Church, and the mission of the Church. Issues that indicate, in fact, the range of themes and challenges faced by John Paul during the long years of his pontificate, and second only to those of the blessed Pius IX. If we were to synthesize into a handy kind of slogan the ministry of this pope – the man who probably met more people in his life than any other in the world, who, even as he was dying did not stop receiving them and almost let himself be worn out by a public that also included so very many young people, who saw in him something that went well beyond the religious aspect – we could say, using his own words, that this man is supremely the way for the Church. A way, as John Paul wrote in his first and programmatic encyclical *Redemptor Hominis* in 1979, "that, in a sense, is the basis of all the other ways that the Church must walk - because man -every man without any exception whatever - has been redeemed by Christ, and because with man - with each man without any exception whatever - Christ is in a way united, even when man is unaware of it: "Christ, who died and was raised up for all, provides man"-each man and every man- "with the light and the strength to measure up to his supreme calling". (14) The insistance of the repetition is evident: every man without any exception whatever, the announcement of a ministry which intended to reach out to every man and to all mankind,

establishing an entirely new style of papal practice in his 104 international journeys and 142 pastoral visits in Italy, uniting the word alone to the symbolic and emotional act of being truly present in almost every part of the world.

Of greatest importance in the mission of John Paul II is the vindication of the self-determination of peoples and nations and the declaration of freedom of thought and religious faith which cast the irresistible seed of emancipation and liberty on the other side of the iron curtain. It was a seed that rapidly put down roots in Poland with the advent of the first free trade union, and culminated in 1989 with the fall of the Berlin Wall and all the communist regimes of eastern Europe. Historians and commentators are unanimous in recognizing the decisive contribution that John Paul made to bringing about this clamourous event. "The events of 1989", he wrote in his social encyclical *Centesimus Annus* in 1991, "are an example of the success of willingness to negotiate and of the Gospel spirit in the face of an adversary determined not to be bound by moral principles. These events are a warning to those who, in the name of political realism, wish to banish law and morality from the political arena." (25) The battle on behalf of the rights of man was not however, to be settled by the transformations that took place in eastern Europe alone, but proceeded courageously to reveal the hidden contradictions within the economic system of the west as well, not to mention the dramatic and intolerable inequality and injustice that divide the north and south of the globe, continually denounced during the 2000 Jubilee. For years the same struggle was focussed on the creation of the European Union, in the firm hope that its Constitution would refer to Christian values and traditions. Lastly and equally fundamental is the heart-felt defence of peace and condemnation of war, never before so explicitly expressed and on which the last energies of his pontificate were concentrated. Appeals that were barely heeded by the world powers but which clearly – especially at the time of the war in Iraq – negated the theory by which the conflict was interpreted as a war between religions. With John Paul II, Catholicism began to refute the notion of violent confrontation with which it had, however,

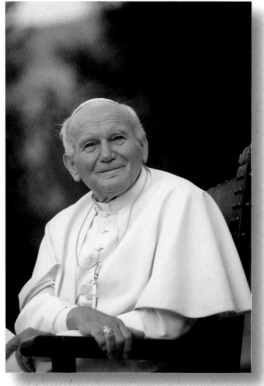

been identified in the previous centuries. In line with the precepts of the Council the papacy of John Paul II paid particular attention to ecumenical and inter-religious dialogue, with words and actions that brought about a new practice of prayer and communion. The joint meetings of many religions in Assisi clearly indicated a point of no return also for the positive global reaction of religions to the phenomenon of globalization. Yet this was not all, for the Church also reaffirmed the role of women to whom John Paul dedicated particular attention in various documents using words that remain fixed in the collective memory, "The Church gives thanks for all the manifestations of the feminine "genius" which have appeared in the course of history, in the midst of all peoples and nations; she gives thanks for all the charisms which the Holy Spirit distributes to women in the history of the People of God, for all the victories which she owes to their faith, hope and charity: she gives thanks for all the fruits of feminine holiness." (*Mulieris Dignitatem*, 31) Yet another concept that concerned the ministry of John Paul was the promotion and recognition of Christian holiness, seen as the credible and successful expression of the glory of a life of faith devoted to the Gospel. "The ways of holiness are many," he wrote in the *Novo Millennio Ineunte*, "according to the vocation of each individual. I thank the Lord that in these years he has enabled me to beatify and canonize a large number of Christians, and among them many lay people who attained holiness in the most ordinary circumstances of life. The time has come to re-propose wholeheartedly to everyone this high standard of ordinary Christian living: the whole life of the Christian community and of Christian families must lead in this direction." The 482 new saints and the 1338 Blessed proclaimed by John Paul II are not therefore an act of mere Christian self-congratulation, but rather an ardent invitation to attempt, with courage and faith, a more demanding devotion to Jesus Christ. Thus John Paul intended to renew the call made to all people of goodwill at the beginning of his pontificate, "Do not be afraid. Open wide the doors for Christ."

Perhaps one of the most surprising acts of the entire pontificate took place during the course of the 2000

Jubilee. It was exactly the frequently announced request for forgiveness, by which the Church, in the person of its universal Pastor, wished to recognise and fully accept its own responsibilities and historic faults and errors. It was an act that was not unanimously approved, but without doubt represented a turning point and an opening to fertile dialogue and hope for the future, "This request for pardon," the Pope affirmed on the eve of the Jubilee, "must not be understoood as an expression of false humility or as a denial of her 2,000-year history, which is certainly richly deserving in the areas of charity, culture and holiness. Instead she responds to a necessary requirement of the truth, which, in addition to the positive aspects, recognizes the human limitations and weaknesses of the various generations of Christ's disciples."

"Sentinels of the morning", "the hope of the Church", "my hope" - with this unique crescendo of regard and affection John Paul II established a privileged relationship with youth, frequently rallied for the World Youth Days invented by himself and subsequently celebrated in almost every continent. The Pope who introduced the third millennium entrusted to youth the task of bringing and announcing Christ to the new era of the Church. "Sometimes when we look at the young, the Pope wrote commenting on the World Youth Day held in Rome, "with the problems and weaknesses that characterize them in contemporary society, we tend to be pessimistic. The Jubilee of Young People however changed that, telling us that young people, whatever their possible ambiguities, have a profound longing for those genuine values which find their fullness in Christ." (*Novo Millennio Ineunte*, 9).

During his ministry, there have been, in fact, many other ideas, tasks and requests that John Paul II wished to fulfil – from important teachings on the mercy of God, the Holy Ghost, the relationship between faith and reason, the lay community, on the missionary work of the Church, that in the 20th century has sadly seen so many new martyrs, to the brief but intense *Letter to Artists*, of 4 April 1999, in which the Pope somehow synthesized his vocation as a writer and poet in a dialogue with those who, through their creative ability, in a certain sense experience the creative anguish of God himself. But there is no doubt that the final years of this papacy, characterised by illness and suffering – never hidden, never denied, and ending at last with the serene decision to go to the Father that he had always served in body and spirit – have more than anything left us with a magnificent lesson of human life, of its unequalled dignity and greatness, its absolute supremacy over any other logic or interest. In fact, the battle to defend life was for John Paul II and still is for us today one of the most sensitive areas in the defence of man. Ideally, he wished to entrust this to Mary, Mother of God and Our Lady, to whom, right from the start he had dedicated his pontificate with the frequently mentioned "Totus tuus". By so doing he also entrusted to her the future of Christians and of the world, "O Mary, bright dawn of the new world, Mother of the living, to you do we entrust the cause of life. Look down, O Mother, upon the vast numbers of babies not allowed to be born, of the poor whose lives are made difficult, of men and women who are victims of brutal violence, of the elderly and the sick killed by indifference or out of misguided mercy. Grant that all who believe in your Son may proclaim the Gospel of life with honesty and love to the people of our time. Obtain for them the grace to accept that Gospel as a gift ever new, the joy of celebrating it with gratitude throughout their lives and the courage to bear witness to it resolutely, in order to build, together with all people of good will, the civilization of truth and love." (*Evangelium Vitae*, 25 March 1995, 105)

The Community of San Leolino

A STORY, A MODEL

Born in Wadowice some 50 kilometres from Krakow, on 18 May 1920, Karol Josef Wojtyla was the third child of an army officer, Karol, and Emilia Kaczorowska. He never knew his sister as she died before he was born and, when he was still very young, his mother too died on 13 April 1929 leaving an unbearable void in the life of little Lolek (as he was nicknamed), yet also a profound need to love and satisfy the affection of a son.

In 1932 his brother Edmund, a doctor, contracted an infection in hospital that lead to his death. The 12 year-old Karol remained alone, therefore, with his father (who was to die in 1941) by now so deeply afflicted by such intolerable loss and sorrow that he increasingly sought refuge in prayer thus providing an early and important example in the life of the future pope.

On completing his schooling in 1938, Karol moved with his father to Krakow to attend the Jagiellonian University. But in September 1939 the Nazi invasion of Poland was to change the lives of himself and his fellow Poles with the devastating force of a terrrible disaster. During the following years, Wojtyla lived through important and formative experiences: to avoid deportation he worked as a labourer in the Solvay chemical industry, at the same time successfully developing his unusual passion for the theatre, clandestinely performing traditional Polish romantic and patriotic classics. His obvious talent seemed to guarantee him an excellent future, but during this period he was also gradually reaching a decision of a much more demanding nature – that of entering the clandestine seminary that the then archbishop of Krakow, Adam Stefan Sapieha, held in his own house. It was, in fact, Sapieha that first recognised the potential of this versatile young man, a lover of literature and poetry, who had decided to enter the monastic life, yet so at ease in relations with others.

With the war over, on 1 November 1946, Wojtyla was ordained as a priest and was sent to Rome to complete and perfect his theological studies. On returning to Poland, he soon revealed a special ability in creating a relatinship with young people and families, whose lives he followed with paternal care and concern. His devotion to the cult of Mary also became increasingly profound; probably deeply rooted in the first bereavement of his life, it was, however, to evolve into a doctrinal guide of the highest level. A devotee of Our Lady of Czestochowa, deeply attached to his own homeland and

all its history, traditions and destiny, a lover of nature and the beauty of creation where the presence of God shines like a light, Wojtyla – with his firm and clear ideas, increasing support and admiration of young people and unceasing social commitment – begins his inevitable progression. In 1958 he was appointed auxiliary bishop of Krakow, in 1962 he went to Rome where, during the Second Vatican Council his fine talent for theology became evident, in 1964 he was made Archbishop of Krakow and on 28 June 1967 he was made a cardinal by Pope Paul VI. In Poland this was a period of great commitment as the Church of Silence was battling against the communist regime, guided by the charismatic Primate Stefan Wyszynski. And Wojtyla was always in the front line, watched with suspicion by the political heirarchy but greatly loved by his fellow men. In Krakow, the parishes grew larger, new churches appeared even in the most neglected working class areas, and belief was strengthened. Until, after the death of Paul VI and of John Paul I, in October 1978 a new Conclave turns to Wojtyla as the next heir to Peter, taking him far from his beloved country, Poland. More than four centuries after the papacy of Hadrian VI, a foreign pope, a Polish pope. For Wojtyla, for John Paul II it was the beginning of a new journey along the highways of the world.

"And so the most Eminent Cardinals have called a new bishop of Rome.
They have called him from a distant country ... distant.
But always so close for communion in the faith
and in the Christian tradition.
I was afraid to accept the nomination but I have done so in the spirit
of obedience to Our Lord Jesus Christ and in total faith towards his
Mother, the most Holy Virgin.
I do not know if I will communicate well in speaking your – our –
Italian language.
If I make mistakes, then correct me."

First speech from the balcony of St Peter's, 16 October 1978

HABEMUS

PAPAM

Open wide the doors for Christ

"Help the Pope and all those who wish to serve Christ and with Christ's power to serve the human person and the whole of mankind. Do not be afraid. Open wide the doors for Christ. To his saving power open the boundaries of States, economic and political systems, the vast fields of culture, civilization and development. Do not be afraid. Christ knows 'what is in man'. He alone knows it."

Homily at the beginning of the Pontificate, St Peter's Square, 22 October 1978

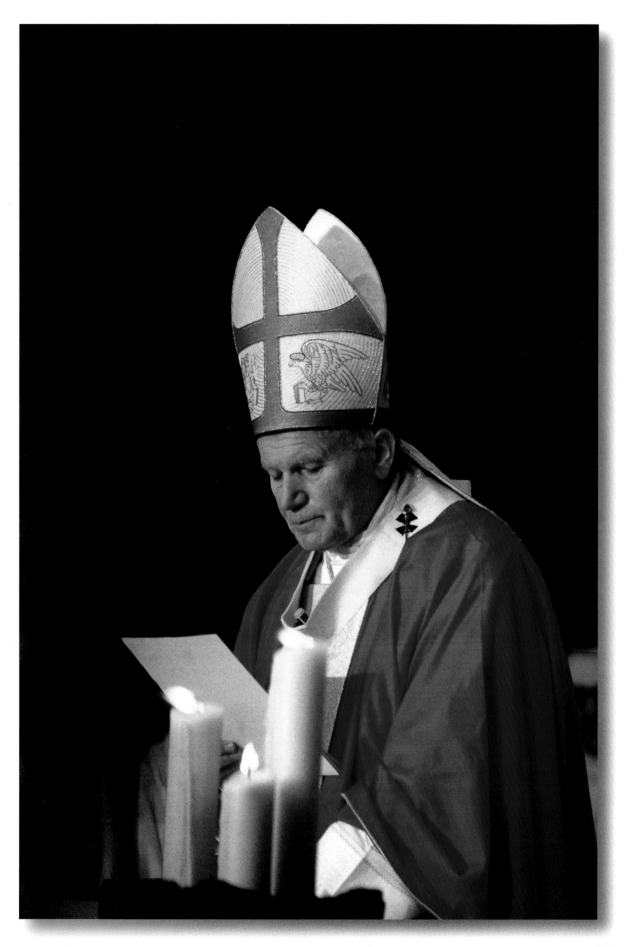

Rome: a new house

"To the See of Peter
in Rome there succeeds
today
a Bishop who is not a
Roman.
A Bishop who is a son of
Poland.
But from this moment he
too becomes a Roman.
Yes—a Roman.
He is a Roman also
because he is the son
of a nation whose history,
from its first dawning,
and whose thousand-
year-old traditions
are marked by a living,
strong, unbroken and
deeply felt link
with the See of Peter,
a nation which has ever
remained faithful
to this See of Rome.
Inscrutable is the design
of Divine Providence!"

*Homily at the beginning of the
Pontificate,
St Peter's Square,
22 October 1978*

"It is here, at the feet of this marvellous Sistine profusion of colour
that the Cardinals gather—

...

And once more Michelangelo wraps them in his vision.

...

The Sistine painting will then speak with the Word of the Lord.

...

It is necessary that during the Conclave, Michelangelo teach them."

John Paul II, Roman Triptych, "Epilogue"

The Globe-trotter Pope

"I am the successor of Peter, but also of Saint Paul, who, to spread the Gospel, was always traveling the world."

The man of communication – Church unity and the great religions

"How good it is, how pleasant,
where the people dwell as one!"

Psalm 133, 1

Our Elder Brothers

"The Jewish religion is not 'extrinsic' to us, but in a certain way is 'intrinsic' to our own religion. With Judaism, therefore, we have a relationship that we do not have with any other religion. You are our dearly beloved brothers and, in a certain way, it could be said that you are our elder brothers."

Meeting with the Jewish Community in the Synagogue of Rome, 13 April 1986

Journey to the Holy Land

*"From this place, where the Resurrection was first made known
to the women and then to the Apostles,
I urge all the Church's members to renew their obedience to
the Lord's command to take the Gospel to all the ends of the earth."*

*Homily in the Church of the Holy Sepulchre
in Jerusalem, 26 March 2000*

"God of our fathers,
you chose Abraham and his descendants
to bring your Name to the Nations:
we are deeply saddened by the behaviour of those
who in the course of history
have caused these children of yours to suffer,
and asking your forgiveness we wish to commit ourselves
to genuine brotherhood
with the people of the Covenant.
We ask this through Christ our Lord.
Amen"

Prayer of the Holy Father
at the Western Wall, Jerusalem,
26 March 2000

With the humblest

...and the famous

Prayer

*"Prayer should accompany the journey of missionaries so that the
proclamation of the word will be effective
through God's grace.
In his Letters, St. Paul often asks the faithful
to pray for him so that he might proclaim
the Gospel with confidence and conviction."*

John Paul II, Redemptoris Missio, 78

Silence

"I have always held the conviction that
if I want to satisfy this inner hunger in others,
I must, following the example of Mary,
first listen to the word of God and mediate it in my heart."

John Paul II, Let us arise and go!

The new millennium: Jubilee 2000

*"Let us go forward in hope!
A new millennium is
opening before the Church
like a vast ocean upon which
we shall venture, relying
on the help of Christ."*

John Paul II,
Novo Millennio Ineunte, 58

*"Holy Spirit, most welcome
guest of our hearts,
reveal to us the profound
meaning of the Great Jubilee
and prepare our hearts to
celebrate it with faith, in
the hope which does not
disappoint,
in the love which seeks nothing
in return."*

John Paul II,
Come, Spirit of love and peace! 1–5

CREATION

"The undulating wood slopes down to the rhythm of mountain streams. To me this rhythm is revealing You, the Primordial Word."

John Paul II, Roman Triptych, "Wonderment"

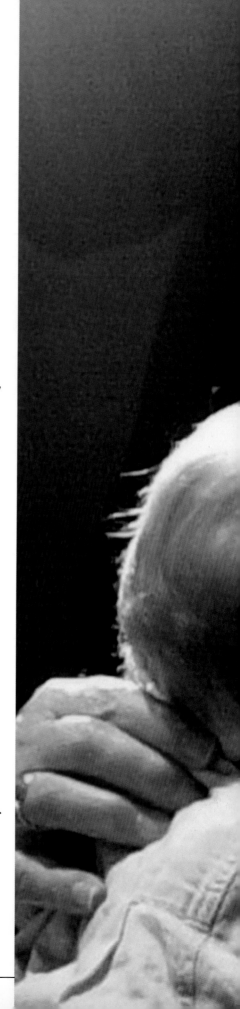

The Pope
and children

*"Raise your tiny hand, Divine Child,
and bless these young friends of yours,
bless the children of all the earth."*

*"Dear children,
Christmas is the feast day of a Child, of a Newborn Baby.
So it is your feast day too! You wait impatiently for it and
get ready for it with joy, counting the days and even the
hours to the Holy Night of Bethlehem.
Dear children, as I write to you I am thinking of when
many years ago I was a child like you. I too used to experience the peaceful feelings of Christmas, and when the
star of Bethlehem shone, I would hurry to the Crib together
with the other boys and girls to relive what happened 2000
years ago in Palestine. We children expressed our joy mostly
in song. How beautiful and moving are the Christmas car-
ols which in the tradition of every people are sung around
the Crib! What deep thoughts they contain, and above all
what joy and tenderness they express about the Divine
Child who came into the world that Holy Night!
In children there is something that must never be missing
in people who want to enter the kingdom of heaven. People who are destined to go to heaven are simple like children, and like children are full of trust, rich in goodness and
pure. Only people of this sort can find in God a Father and,
thanks to Jesus, can become in their own turn children of
God."*

Letter to Children, 13 December 1994

54

Youth, the sentinels of the morning

"The first appeal I want to address to you,
young men and women of today, is this:
Do not be afraid!
Do not be afraid of your own youth,
and of those deep desires
you have for happiness, for truth, for beauty
and for lasting love!
Sometimes people say that society is
afraid of these powerful desires of young people,
and that you yourselves are afraid of them.
Do not be afraid!
When I look at you, the young people,
I feel great gratitude and hope.
The future far into the next century lies
in your hands.
The future of peace lies in your hearts.
To construct history, as you can and must,
you must free history from
the false paths it is pursuing."

Message for the XVIII World Day of Peace,
1 January 1985

"Here I wish to express my most heartfelt gratitude to God for the gift of youthfulness that, through you, remains in the Church and the world.

I also wish to give God fervent thanks for allowing me to accompany the youth of the world for the last two decades of the century that has just ended, showing them the way that leads to Christ, 'the same yesterday and today and forever' (Heb 13:8). But, at the same time, I thank God because the young people have accompanied and almost supported the Pope during his apostolic pilgrimages around the world.

Therefore, do not be afraid to walk the way first trodden by the Lord. With your youthfulness, put your mark of hope and enthusiasm, so typical of your age, on the third millennium that is just beginning. If you allow the grace of God to work in you, and earnestly fulfill this commitment daily, you will make this new century a better time for everyone."

Message for the XVI World Youth Day, 14 February 2001

"Totus tuus"

"Behold, your mother!" (Jn 19,27)

"This is why I now wish to repeat the motto of my episcopal and pontifical service: 'Totus tuus'. Throughout my life I have experienced the loving and forceful presence of the Mother of Our Lord. Mary accompanies me every day in the fulfilment of my mission as Successor of Peter."

Message for the XVIII World Youth Day, 13 April 2003

A LIFE AND A PROPHECY

There are men who seem to have an exact path to follow, who seem to devote their lives to destiny's greater design. There are men who are predestined and Karol Wojtyla was clearly one of these. He wanted to be an actor, he was young, attractive, strong, extrovert, but a powerful vocation lead him towards the seminary. He wanted to retire to a monastery to lead a life of contemplation, but yet again, other and different plans awaited him and his path lead towards Rome, then to the bishopric of Krakow, then the Council and again to Krakow as a cardinal.

When the seat of Peter became a possibility and then a reality, legendary prophecies were remembered: Sister Faustina Kowalska, a Polish mystic dear to the young Wojtyla and later canonized by him, had predicted that a great sun would rise from Poland to illuminate the destinies of the Church and the world, while Padre Pio (Father Pius), also canonized by John Paul II, had recognised a future pope in the young Wojtyla. Yet another even greater prophecy was to affect the life of the Pope – the mystery concealed in the third secret of Fatima, which recognised him as the Father destined to fall under a burst of gunfire, but also to rise again to restore, finally and definitively, Russia to the Immaculate Heart of Mary, changing the fate of the world. And there it all was: the attack of 1981, the fall of the Berlin Wall in 1989, and Russia dedicated to the Virgin Mary. This was the Virgin to whom

the Pope had entirely devoted himself, in whom he had found the adored mother he had lost too early, and for whom he had attended the public recitation of the Rosary on the first Saturday of every month. This was a special devotion, for the Madonna of Fatima had made a promise: to all those who observed this act she guaranteed her maternal presence and heavenly welcome at the moment of death, which would take place on the first Saturday of the month. Karol Wojtyla died on the 2nd of April, the first Saturday of the month, after vespers at the beginning of a new liturgical day, the first day of the celebration of Saint Faustina Kowalska.

THE ASSASSINATION ATTEMPT

S aint Peter's Square, General Audience, 13 May 1981, at 5.17 pm. Pope John Paul II fell to the ground, shot by Mehmet Ali Agca. He arrived at the nearby Gemelli Polyclinic having almost bled to death and only a lengthy and complex surgical operation would manage to save his life. One might say it was a miracle.

Karol Wojtyla was quick to identify the source of inspiration for that miracle, strengthening, if that were possible, his fervent devotion to the Virgin Mary. For the church, 13 May is dedicated to the Holy Virgin of Fatima, and it was in the third secret revealed to the shepherds of Fatima that a white bishop was mentioned, who would fall by sacrilegious violence. A 'motherly hand' therefore intervened to deviate the bullet, a bullet that in gratitude the Pope had set in the splendid crown

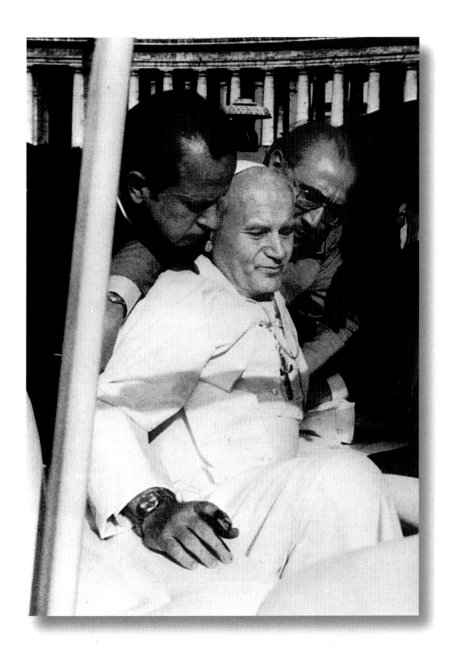

of the miraculous Virgin, in a gesture of profound homage.
The Pope himself affirmed the unshakeable and confident
certainty of divine intervention in the homily for the
beatification of the shepherds Jacinta and Francesco, delivered
during his journey to Fatima on 13 May 2000.
"Here in Fátima, where these times of tribulation were
foretold and Our Lady asked for prayer and penance to
shorten them, I would like today to thank heaven for the
powerful witness shown in all those lives. And once again
I would like to celebrate the Lord's goodness to me when
I was saved from death after being gravely wounded on 13
May 1981. I also express my gratitude to Bl. Jacinta for the
sacrifices and prayers offered for the Holy Father, whom she
saw suffering greatly."

The shepherd

"*I am the good shepherd,
and I know mine
and mine know me,
just as the Father knows
me and I know
the Father;
and I will lay down
my life
for the sheep.*"

John, 10, 14

"I have other sheep that do not belong to this fold. These also I must lead,
and they will hear my voice, and there will be one flock, one shepherd."

John, 10, 16

The Paradise of
John Paul II

*In 26 and a half years of his pontificate, the Holy Father proclaimed
428 saints and 1338 Blessed*

Grief throughout the world

"The joys and the hopes, the griefs and the anxieties of the men of this age, especially those who are poor or in any way afflicted, these are the joys and hopes, the griefs and anxieties of the followers of Christ. Indeed, nothing genuinely human fails to raise an echo in their hearts."

Paul VI, Gaudium et Spes, 1

"Declaring the power of salvific suffering, the Apostle Paul says: 'In my flesh I complete what is lacking in Christ's afflictions for the sake of his body, that is, the Church'."

John Paul II, Salvifici Doloris, 1

"Every threat to human dignity and life must necessarily be felt in the Church's very heart; it cannot but affect her at the core of her faith."

John Paul II, Evangelium Vitae, 3

"Although the world of today has a very vivid awareness of its unity and of how one man depends on another in needful solidarity, it is most grievously turn into opposing camps by conflicting forces. For political, social, economic, racial and ideological disputes still continue bitterly, and with them the peril of a war which would reduce everything to ashes."

Paul VI, Gaudium et Spes, 4

The man of peace

"Dear Brothers and Sisters,
I have invited Catholics to take part in a day of fasting next Friday,
14 December, to implore God for a stable peace that is based on justice.
This initiative has also found support among the faithful of other religions,
particularly Jews and Muslims, as well as among many persons of good will.

In today's complex international situation, humanity is called to mobilize its
best energies so that love may prevail over hatred, peace over war, truth over
falsehood and forgiveness over revenge.

Moreover, the date of 14 December coincides with the end of Ramadan,
during which the followers of Islam express their submission to the One
God through fasting. I fervently hope that our common attitude of religious
repentance will increase reciprocal understanding between
Christians and Muslims who are called, today more than ever,
to build justice and peace together."

Angelus, Second Sunday of Advent, 9 December 2001

In the Autumn of Life

"Despite the limitations brought on by age, I continue to enjoy life. For this
I thank the Lord. It is wonderful to be able to give oneself to the very end
for the sake of the Kingdom of God! At the same time, I find great peace in
thinking of the time when the Lord will call me: from life to life!
And so I often find myself saying, with no trace of melancholy,
a prayer recited by priests after the celebration of the Eucharist: 'In hora
mortis meae voca me, et iube me venire ad te' –
at the hour of my death, call me and bid me come to you.
This is the prayer of Christian hope, which in no way detracts from the joy of
the present, while entrusting the future to God's gracious and loving care.
'Iube me venire ad te!': this is the deepest yearning of the human heart, even
in those who are not conscious of it. Grant, O Lord of life, that we may be
ever vividly aware of this and that we may savour every season of our lives
as a gift filled with promise for the future.
Grant that we may lovingly accept your will,
and place ourselves each day in your merciful hands. And when the moment
of our definitive 'passage' comes, grant that we may face it with serenity,
without regret for what we shall leave behind."

Letter to the elderly, 1 October 1999

THE VATICAN CITY

2 APRIL 2005 – 9.37 PM

The last embrace

PICTURE CAPTIONS

p. 5
John Paul II on a pastoral visit to Fiesole.

p. 8
A young Karol Wojtyla with his mother.

p. 9
Above, Wojtyla as a baby with his parents and, below, as a young priest whose dynamic non-conformity is already evident.

p. 10-11
Wojtyla as a cardinal: below, Paul VI imposes the cardinal's biretta in 1967.

pp. 12-13
Just elected Pope, Wojtyla comes to the balcony of St Peter's Square on 16 October 1978.

p. 16
The Pope in Sicily in 1993.

pp. 18-19
The pastoral visit to Fiesole: Bishop Luciano Giovannetti stands to the right of the Pope.

p. 22
Ceremony in the Sistine Chapel on 7 April 1994.

p. 24
Above, an innovation for the travels of John Paul II: the 'Pope Mobile'. Below, the Pope arrives in Cochabamba, in Bolivia to celebrate mass on 11 May 1988.

p. 25
The Pope's visit to Papua New Guinea, 8 May 1984.

p. 26
The Pope in Jerusalem at the Wailing Wall 26 March 2000.

p. 27
Jerusalem, at the Holy Cenacle during the journey to the Holy Land.

p. 28
The meeting with the Dalai Lama, 28 October 1999.

p. 29
The journey to the Holy Land: at the Omar Mosque, 26 March 2000.

p. 30-31
The historic meeting with the Chief Rabbi of Rome, Elio Toaff, at the Synagogue of Rome, 14 April 1986.

p. 32
Jerusalem, at the Holy Cenacle during the journey to the Holy Land.

p. 33
The journey to the Holy Land: the Pope at the Holy Sepulchre.

p. 34
Above, visit to Gethsemane; below, in prayer at the Holy Sepulchre.

p. 35
Above, at the Stone of the Annointing in the Holy Sepulchre in Jerusalem; below, another image of the visit to the Holy Sepulchre.

p. 36
Worshipping the image of the Baby Jesus in Bethlehem, at the Grotto of the Nativity, 22 March 2000.

p. 37
The Pope at the Wailing Wall, Jerusalem, 26 March 2000.

p. 38
An indigenous woman praying in Guatamala City, during the Paope's mass on 30 July 2002.

p. 39
Above, the Pope wearing an Indian headdress in a ceremony in Ontario (Canada), 15 September 1984. Below, a crowd of the faithful carrying chairs as they go to the Pope's mass at Onitsha, in Nigeria 22 March 1998.

pp. 40-41
Historic meetings: from above left, with Fidel Castro in Havana, 25 January 1998; with Yasser Arafat, during his journey to the Holy Land in 2000; with Bill Clinton on arrival in the United States, 4 October 1995; with Mikhail Gorbaciov, the Soviet president, in the Vatican on 1 December 1989.

p. 42
Solemn inauguration of the Holy Year, 25 March 1983.

p. 44
Above, the Pope in prayer; below, in Bethlehem at the Grotto of the Nativity, 22 March 2000.

p. 45
In the Holy Land, visiting the Holy Sepulchre, in Jerusalem.

pp. 46-47
The land of Abraham, from Mount Nebo, during the journey to the Holy Land in 2000.

pp. 48-51
Images of the ceremony held at the opening of the Holy Year, 2000.

p. 56
The Pope releases doves of peace from the window of his private apartment, 30 January 2005.

p. 57
Above, a child listens attentively to the Pope's mass for the canonization of the missionary Pedro de San Josè Betencur, in Guatemala City, 30 July 2002. Below, the Pope kisses a young girl in Ilopango, in Salvador, 8 February 1996.

p. 59
The Pope responds to the warm welcome given by young people at Madison Square Garden in New York, 3 October 1979.

p. 60
The Pope surrounded by children in Ukraine, 23 June 2001.

p. 61
World Youth Day in Paris, 21 August 1997.

p. 62
The Pope in prayer in the Massabielle Cave in Lourdes, 14 August 1983.

p. 63
The journey to the Holy Land: visiting the Holy Sepulchre in Jerusalem.

p. 64
Praying before the Madonna of Fatima in May 1982.

p. 65
Perhaps the religious image most dear to the heart of John Paul II – Our Lady of Czestochowa, during his first return trip to Poland in June 1979.

pp. 66-67
Triumphal visit to Fatima on 13 May 1982.

p. 68
Above, the statue of the Madonna of Fatima and an image of her precious crown where, as a sign of gratitude, John Paul II had set the bullet that wounded him on 13 May 1981, in the attack that took place in St Peter's Square. Below, Fatima, May 1991, the meeting with Sister Lucia, one of the shepherds who experienced the appearance of the Virgin in 1917.

p. 69
An historic photo: the Pope in St Peter's Square on 13 May 1981, immediately before Ali Agca fired at him (on the far left we can see the gun already pointing at the pontiff).

pp. 70-71
The Pope holds little Sarah just before the attack in St Peter's. Once struck, he was supported by the personal secretary, Monsignor Dziwisz, while the vehicle speeds to the nearby Gemelli Polyclinic.

p. 73
The Pope during the Holy Week, 1997.

p. 74
The canonization of Padre Pio (Father Pius) in St Peter's on 16 June 2002.

p. 75
The moving meeting with Mother Theresa of Calcutta in St Peter's Basilica on 29 June 1997. After her death, John Paul II rapidly approved her beatification on 19 October 2003.

pp. 76-77
From above left: the Pope meets invalids at Lourdes; praying in the Holy Land at Gethsemane; a view of Auschwitz.

p. 78
The Pope with the heads of twelve other religions during the World Day of Prayer for Peace, at Santa Maria degli Angeli, Assisi on 27 October 1986.

p. 79
In St Peter's, 10 April 2003: the dove is released as a symbolic token of the numerous calls for peace made by the Pope.

pp. 80-81
The Pope visiting the United Nations, 15 October 1995.

p. 82
A telling image of the elderly pontiff, during the Easter mass, 19 April 2003.

p. 83
Already unwell, the Pope celebrates mass at Guatemala City, 30 July 2002.

p. 84
The Pope in St Louis, 27 January 1999.

p. 85
Guatemala City, 30 July 2002: tiredness is evident on the face of the Pope as he prays.

pp. 90-91
On the afternoon of 4 April 2005, the body of the Pope is solemnly transferred from the 'Clementine Hall' to St Peter's Basilica, where the faithful could pay their last respects.
The procession fills St Peter's Square where an enormous crowd pays homage to the coffin.

pp. 92-94
The funeral in St Peter's on 8 April 2005.

p. 95
Above, the crowd of faithful that attended the funeral of the Pope calls for the beatification of John Paul II.
Below, John Paul's burial place in the Grotto beneath St Peter's Basilica.

This book was compiled in the hours that followed the funeral of John Paul II.

The Publisher would like to thank the editorial staff, the authors, the editors, the graphic artists and all those who contributed to make possible its publication in an exceptionally short time, providing a synthesis of all that has contributed to create the feeling of affection and respect that the world has shown for this great Pope in the almost twenty seven years of his pontificate.

Printed by Centro Stampa Editoriale Bonechi, Sesto Fiorentino (Florence), 11 April 2005